BIG AIR SKATEBOARDING

BY THOMAS K. ADAMSON

EPIC

BELLWETHER MEDIA • MINNEAPOLIS, MN

EPIC BOOKS are no ordinary books. They burst with intense action, high-speed heroics, and shadows of the unknown. Are you ready for an Epic adventure?

This edition first published in 2016 by Bellwether Media, Inc.

No part of this publication may be reproduced in whole or in part without written permission of the publisher. For information regarding permission, write to Bellwether Media, Inc., Attention: Permissions Department, 5357 Penn Avenue South, Minneapolis, MN 55419.

Library of Congress Cataloging-in-Publication Data

Adamson, Thomas K., 1970-
  Big Air Skateboarding / by Thomas K. Adamson.
    pages cm. – (Epic: Extreme Sports)
  Includes bibliographical references and index.
  Summary: "Engaging images accompany information about big air skateboarding. The combination of high-interest subject matter and light text is intended for students in grades 2 through 7"– Provided by publisher.
  Audience: Ages 7 to 12
  ISBN 978-1-62617-272-2 (hardcover: alk. paper)
  1. Skateboarding–Juvenile literature. 2. Extreme sports–Juvenile literature. 3. ESPN X-Games–Juvenile literature. I. Title.
  GV859.8.A426 2016
  796.22–dc23
                    2015001629

Printed in the United States of America, North Mankato, MN.

TABLE OF CONTENTS

WARNING
The tricks shown in this book are performed by professionals. Always wear a helmet and other safety gear when you are on a skateboard.

X GAMES GOLD

   Tom Schaar stands on his skateboard 88 feet (27 meters) above the ground. A strong wind blows in his face.

   Schaar drops in. He speeds down the **steep** ramp. He hits the jump and flies across the gap. He spins around twice to land a 720.

Schaar then launches out of the quarterpipe. He spins two and a half times in the air. He wobbles on the landing. But he stays on his board to complete the 900. The 14-year-old has won X Games gold!

BIG AIR SKATEBOARDING

In big air skateboarding, skaters speed down a ramp higher than some buildings. They reach speeds of up to 55 miles (89 kilometers) per hour! They attempt the longest jumps and highest **tricks** in skateboarding.

FLYING HIGH
A skater might fly 20 feet (6 meters) above the quarterpipe lip. This is actually about 40 feet (12 meters) from the ground!

Daring riders push the limits of the sport. They try tricks no one has done before. Their **style** and **creativity** keep fans watching.

BIG AIR SKATEBOARDING TERMS

720—two full spins in the air

900—two and a half spins in the air

drop in—to begin skating down the launch ramp to start a run

gap—the distance between the launch ramp and the landing ramp

lip—the top of the quarterpipe

MegaRamp—the name of the whole ramp used for big air skateboarding

quarterpipe—a ramp at the end of the MegaRamp that looks like one quarter of a pipe

BIG AIR BEGINNINGS

Danny Way created the ramp used for big air skateboarding in 2002. He called it the MegaRamp. Skaters were amazed at its size. The X Games added the event in 2004.

OFF THE RAILS

For two years, the X Games featured the Big Air Rail Jam. Skaters rode a 20-foot (6-meter) rail across the gap.

CLOSE TO HOME
Skateboarding great Bob Burnquist has a MegaRamp in his backyard.

At first, few skaters were brave enough to ride the MegaRamp. Now, skaters as young as 11 speed down the huge ramp.

BIG AIR GEAR

Big air skateboarding is dangerous. Skateboarders wear pads on their knees, elbows, and hips. Helmets and gloves keep their heads and hands safe. They also wear protectors on their shins, chests, and backs.

MOUTHING OFF
Skaters wear mouth guards for their teeth-rattling crashes.

THE COMPETITION

Skaters compete in **qualifying rounds**. Skaters with the highest scores move on to the next round.

EVENT SCORING

Judges give skaters a score out of 100. They look for style and creativity. They also award more points for bigger air. Landing hard tricks will earn skaters a higher score. Doing a trick no one has ever seen before will also impress the judges.

GOING WAY UP
Sometimes skaters have to ride an elevator to get to the top of the MegaRamp.

Five skaters make it to the final round. Each skater gets five **runs**. Only the best run counts. Skaters have many chances to take risks and do difficult tricks.

INNOVATOR OF THE SPORT

name: Danny Way
birthdate: April 15, 1974
hometown: San Diego, California
innovations: Invented the MegaRamp, used for all X Games Skateboard Big Air competitions

21

GLOSSARY

creativity—having new ideas or doing something a different way

qualifying rounds—early parts of a competition; skaters with the highest scores move through the qualifying rounds.

runs—turns at competing in an event

steep—almost straight up and down

style—the way something is done

tricks—specific moves in a skateboarding event

TO LEARN MORE

AT THE LIBRARY

Craats, Rennay. *Skateboarding*. New York, N.Y.: AV2 by Weigl, 2014.

Otfinoski, Steven. *Extreme Skateboarding*. New York, N.Y.: Marshall Cavendish, 2013.

Polydoros, Lori. *Skateboarding Greats*. Mankato, Minn.: Capstone Press, 2012.

ON THE WEB

Learning more about big air skateboarding is as easy as 1, 2, 3.

1. Go to www.factsurfer.com.

2. Enter "big air skateboarding" into the search box.

3. Click the "Surf" button and you will see a list of related web sites.

With factsurfer.com, finding more information is just a click away.

INDEX